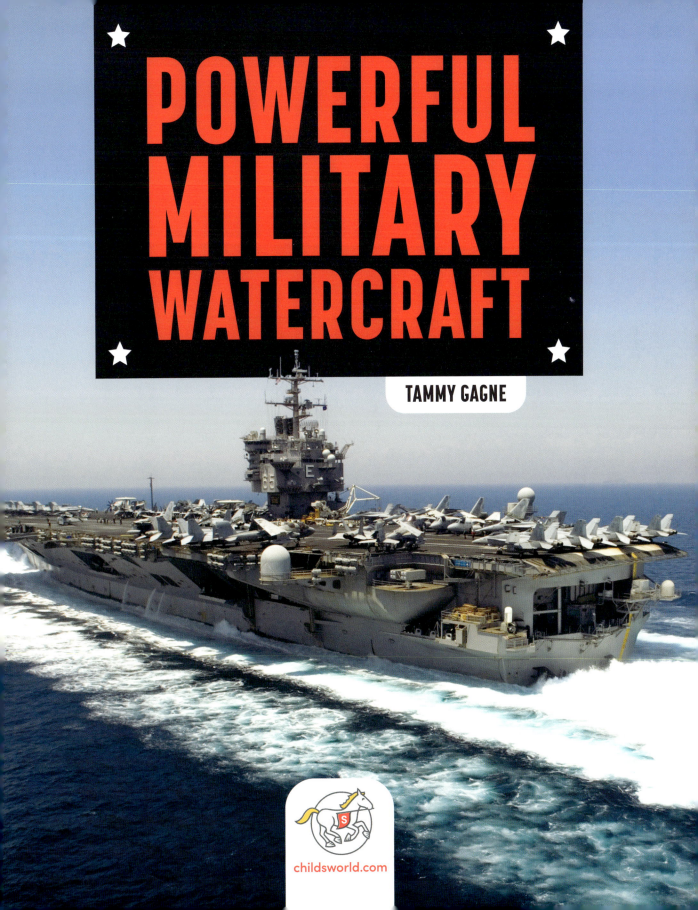

POWERFUL MILITARY WATERCRAFT

TAMMY GAGNE

childsworld.com

Published by The Child's World®
800-599-READ • www.childsworld.com

Photography Credits
Photographs ©: US Navy/DVIDS, cover, 1, 7 (white), 13;
Mass Communication Specialist 3rd Class Bela Chambers/
US Navy, 3; Mass Communication Specialist Seaman
Trent P. Hawkins/US Navy, 5; Petty Officer 3rd Class
Daniel Tillie/US Navy/DVIDS, 7 (blue); Seaman Apprentice
Leonard Adams/US Navy/DVIDS, 7 (green); Petty Officer
3rd Class Christopher Gaines/US Navy/DVIDS, 7 (red);
Mass Communication Specialist 2nd Class Kelsey Trinh/
US Navy, 7 (yellow); Mass Communication Specialist
Seaman Mikesa R. Ponder/US Navy/DVIDS, 7 (purple);
Mass Communications Specialist 2nd Class Jason Isaacs/
US Navy, 9; General Dynamics Bath Iron Works/US
Navy/DVIDS, 10; Mass Communication Specialist 1st
Class Melvin Nobeza/US Navy, 14; Mass Communication
Specialist 2nd Class Alex Perlman/US Navy, 16; Petty
Officer 1st Class Ronald Gutridge/US Navy/DVIDS, 17;
Mass Communication Specialist 2nd Class Caleb Dyal/
US Navy, 19; Chief Mass Communication Specialist Keith
Devinney/US Navy, 20

ISBN Information
9781503816725 (Reinforced Library Binding)
9781503881419 (Portable Document Format)
9781503882720 (Online Multi-user eBook)
9781503884038 (Electronic Publication)

LCCN 2022951209

Printed in the United States of America

ABOUT THE AUTHOR

Tammy Gagne has written hundreds of books for both adults and children. Some of her recent books are about satellites and colonizing Mars. She lives in northern New England with her husband, son, and dogs.

CONTENTS

CHAPTER ONE

READY FOR TAKEOFF

The USS *George Washington* flight crew members can barely hear themselves think. All they can hear are sounds from fighter jet engines. An F-35 Lightning II just launched into the air. An F/A-18 Hornet now prepares to take off. The *George Washington* is an aircraft carrier. It serves as a runway for planes in the US Navy.

The USS *George Washington* measures just 1,092 feet (333 m) long. This is very short for a runway. Pilots and the flight deck crew are trained to make the most of the tight space on aircraft carriers.

Crew members scurry across the deck. They are readying the Hornet for takeoff. Colorful jerseys divide the crew members by their jobs. Officers wearing yellow run a **catapult**. Catapults help planes reach the speed needed for takeoff on such a short runway.

Aircraft reach speeds of about 165 miles per hour (266 kmh) in two seconds when launching from an aircraft carrier.

A crew member in green crouches at the nose of the Hornet. He attaches the plane to the catapult system. He rushes away. Another crew member wearing yellow signals that the plane is ready. Steam fills the runway. The steam powers **pistons** within the catapult system. Crew members watch as the catapult slings the Hornet forward. The aircraft takes off.

Other officers prepare the deck for an incoming ES-3A Shadow. The officers stretch wires made of heavy steel across the carrier's deck. Each plane has a **tailhook**. As the pilot lands the Shadow, its tailhook catches on one of these wires. It brings the aircraft to a stop in just seconds.

The USS *George Washington* is one of many aircraft carriers in the US Navy. It can carry up to 90 aircraft at one time. Aircraft carriers are among the most powerful watercraft the military uses.

There are lots of crew members on an aircraft carrier. Each person wears a specific color to show what his or her job is.

JERSEY COLORS ON AIRCRAFT CARRIERS

Crew members in blue run forklifts and tractors.

Crew members in green perform maintenance on planes and run launch systems.

Crew members in red load missiles and other ammunition onto planes.

Crew members in yellow direct planes and support the launch process.

Crew members in purple put fuel in planes.

Crew members in white make sure all systems are safe on the carrier.

CHAPTER TWO

DESTROYERS

Destroyers help the US Navy defend against attacks in war. These combat ships operate from the ocean's surface. But their defense systems can strike enemies in the water, in the air, and even on land.

Arleigh Burke–class ships are the most powerful class of US Navy destroyers. Each ship can carry a variety of deadly weapons. These include the MK-45 5-inch gun. It can strike nearby ships or aircraft. Arleigh Burke destroyers also have six MK-46 **torpedoes**. These underwater weapons can sink enemy submarines. Arleigh Burke ships are also armed with Tomahawk missiles. These missiles can travel up to 1,000 miles (1,610 km) to strike land targets.

Arleigh Burke ships can also carry two helicopters. These aircraft can launch weapons at enemy ships or aircraft. Some helicopters can also find, track, and attack submarines.

The MK-45 5-inch gun is near the front of an Arleigh Burke–class ship.

In 2016, the USS *Zumwalt* became the largest destroyer in the US Navy. It is 610 feet (186 m) long. It is about 100 feet (30 m) longer than Arleigh Burke destroyers. The USS *Zumwalt* is also more advanced than other destroyers. It has 80 missile-launching tubes. They can shoot missiles at targets in the air or the water. They can even shoot down incoming enemy missiles.

This ship looks different from any other in naval history. The *Zumwalt*'s hull, or exterior, has sharp corners and a narrow deck, unlike previous destroyers. This **stealthy** design makes it more difficult for enemy **radar** to detect Zumwalt-class destroyers.

HYPERSONIC WEAPONS

The US Navy plans to replace the main guns on the USS *Zumwalt* with up to 12 hypersonic missiles. Hypersonic missiles are very powerful. They can fly five times the speed of sound. That's more than 3,800 miles per hour (6,120 kmh). They are some of the fastest weapons in the world, so it is difficult to defend against them.

Some people describe the shape of the USS Zumwalt *as looking like a knife cutting through the water.*

CHAPTER THREE

SUBMARINES

Submarines are military watercraft that travel far below the ocean's surface. The US Navy uses three types of submarines: attack submarines, ballistic submarines, and guided missile submarines. All are used in combat. Attack submarines are armed with torpedoes. The subs can use these weapons to attack enemy ships from underwater. Virginia-class submarines can carry up to 65 torpedoes.

Virginia submarines are known for being stealthy. Subs are made to spend most of their time underwater where the surroundings are dark. Being so deep helps them hide from enemies. But subs must also be quiet to remain unnoticed.

Even when a submarine comes to the surface, much of the sub stays underwater.

Sailors attach a submarine to the submarine
tender while the sub is resupplied.

Submarines are loudest when they are moving. The faster they go, the louder they become. Most subs use a large **propeller** to help move the craft through the water. This device can make a lot of noise. But Virginia subs don't use propellers. Instead, they have pump-jet propulsion systems. These subs use a jet of water to push the craft forward.

Virginia-class submarines are among the quietest in the world. The average noise of the ocean measures about 90 **decibels**. Virginia subs are just slightly louder at about 95 decibels. They can travel much faster than other submarines while remaining stealthy.

SUBMARINE TENDERS

Most submarine missions last for months at a time. A sub remains hundreds of feet underwater in the middle of an ocean for most of its mission. Submarines store lots of food. They have systems for creating oxygen on board. They can also turn seawater into fresh drinking water. When a submarine crew needs important supplies, a ship called a submarine tender delivers them.

A Virginia-class submarine can travel more than 28 miles per hour (45 kmh) while underwater.

Ballistic missile submarines are the most powerful subs. Also called boomers, they are armed with **intercontinental** ballistic missiles. These missiles have a range of about 3,400 miles (5,470 km). They carry nuclear weapons. Before 2010, each of the US Navy's Ohio-class submarines could carry up to 24 of these submarine-launched ballistic weapons. But the United States made an agreement with Russia to reduce the total to 20 weapons per sub.

The US Navy also has four guided missile submarines. These submarines fire nonnuclear weapons. They can each carry up to 154 Tomahawk missiles. Guided missile submarines are made to attack targets on land. Together, these three types of subs allow the US Navy to be prepared for any type of combat.

Submarines can launch ballistic missiles and Tomahawk missiles from underwater.

CHAPTER FOUR

AIRCRAFT CARRIERS

Aircraft carriers are like floating air bases. Crew members fill aircraft with fuel and load ammunition. They fix and maintain the aircraft. Once the aircraft are ready, pilots take off from the carrier.

Aircraft carriers serve an important role during times of war. Their aircraft carry out critical missions. Some aircraft protect the carrier itself and other ships nearby. Others gather information about an enemy. This information helps the military plan successful missions.

Many people are needed to do all the work performed on an aircraft carrier. For example, the USS *Nimitz* has a crew of about 5,000 people. Some of these crew members work with the aircraft. Others perform important duties such as food service and medical care. This carrier also has its own gym and library. It even has a dentist's office.

The USS Ronald Reagan is a Nimitz-class aircraft carrier. It can fit up to 90 aircraft on board.

US Navy watercraft work together to keep the United States safe.

Modern aircraft carriers use nuclear energy. This energy allows them to run for more than ten years before refueling. These city-like ships make it possible for the US Navy to operate from almost anywhere in the world.

Watercraft are an essential part of the US Navy. These ships can attack enemies on water, in the air, or on land with many kinds of weapons. Aircraft carriers even provide moveable military bases. Whether the US Navy's watercraft are traveling on top of the water or deep under the ocean, they are a powerful addition to the US military.

GLOSSARY

catapult (KAT-uh-pult) A catapult is a device that is used to help aircraft take off from a short runway. The flight deck crew used the catapult to help the fighter jet return to the air.

decibels (DEH-suh-belz) Decibels are units of measurement for sound. Noise on an aircraft carrier can reach 150 decibels.

intercontinental (in-tur-kon-tuh-NEN-tuhl) Intercontinental describes something that can travel from one continent to another. Some submarines carry intercontinental ballistic missiles.

pistons (PIST-unz) Pistons are solid cylinders that slide up and down inside metal tubes to create motion. The pistons used energy from steam to help the catapult launch the fighter jet.

propeller (pruh-PEH-lur) A propeller has rotating blades that turn underwater to move an object forward. The submarine's propeller spun quickly as the watercraft moved along the ocean floor.

radar (RAY-dar) Radar is a system of equipment that sends out signals and then detects the reflections of those signals after they bounce off objects. Militaries use radar to detect enemy watercraft.

stealthy (STEL-thee) Stealthy describes something that is designed not to be seen or heard. The stealthy ship traveled through the water unnoticed by the enemy's radar.

tailhook (TAYL-hook) A tailhook is a device on an aircraft that helps it stop quickly when landing. The plane's tailhook caught on the wire stretched across the aircraft carrier's deck.

torpedoes (tor-PEE-dohz) Torpedoes are missiles that are fired underwater from a ship or submarine. The submarine fired several torpedoes at the enemy watercraft.

FAST FACTS

★ The US military uses watercraft to attack enemies and to defend its own ships.

★ Destroyers are combat ships that can launch weapons from the ocean's surface. These weapons can strike enemies in the water, in the air, or on land.

★ Submarines spend most of their time far below the water's surface. They can launch weapons at enemy subs or at ships on the surface. They can also launch missiles into the air. Many subs are equipped with long-range nuclear weapons.

★ Aircraft carriers provide the US Navy with a place to launch and land aircraft at sea.

ONE STRIDE FURTHER

★ The most modern US Navy destroyers are designed to avoid enemy radar. How might this be helpful in combat?

★ Submarines are usually on missions for long periods of time. The crews remain deep underwater away from society. What challenges do you think sailors aboard these watercraft face? How do you think they deal with these challenges?

★ Aircraft carriers provide pilots with a portable runway in the middle of the ocean. Landing on aircraft carriers can be difficult. What skills do you think would be important for navy pilots to have?

FIND OUT MORE

IN THE LIBRARY

Koran, Maria. *The U.S. Navy.* New York, NY:
Lightbox Learning, Inc., 2022.

Ransom, Candice. *How Aircraft Carriers Work.*
Minneapolis, MN: Lerner Publications, 2020.

Swanson, Jennifer. *How Do Submarines Work?*
Parker, CO: The Child's World, 2022.

ON THE WEB

Visit our website for links about military watercraft:
childsworld.com/links

Note to Parents, Caregivers, Teachers, and Librarians: We routinely verify our Web links to make sure they are safe and active sites. So encourage your readers to check them out!

INDEX